About Fish

A Guide for Children

Cathryn Sill

Illustrated by John Sill

PEACHTREE

ATLANTA

For the One who created fish.
—*Genesis* 1:1

Published by
PEACHTREE PUBLISHING COMPANY INC.
1700 Chattahoochee Avenue
Atlanta, Georgia 30318-2112
www.peachtree-online.com

Text © 2002, 2017 Cathryn P. Sill
Jacket and interior illustrations © 2002, 2017 John C. Sill

First trade paperback edition published 2005

First bilingual edition published in 2017

Illustrations painted in watercolor on archival quality 100% rag watercolor paper
Text and titles typeset in Novarese from Adobe Systems

Edited by Vicky Holifield

Printed in September 2019 by Toppan Leefung Printing Limited in China
10 9 8 7 6 5 4 3 2 1 (hardcover edition)
10 9 8 7 6 5 4 (trade paperback edition)

HC ISBN: 978-1-56145-987-2
PB ISBN: 978-1-56145-988-9

Also available in bilingual edition
PB: 978-1-56145-989-6

Library of Congress Cataloging-in-Publication Data

Sill, Cathryn P., 1953– author.
About fish : a guide for children / written by Cathryn Sill ; illustrated by John Sill.—1st ed.
p. cm.
Summary: Introduces various species of fish, describing their food needs, body structures, protective mechanisms, habitats, and reproduction.
ISBN 1-56145-256-4
I. Fishes—Juvenile literature. [1. Fishes.] I. Sill, John, II. Title.
QL617.2 .S56 2002
597—dc21
2001005568

About Fish

Fish live in water all over the world.

PLATE 1
Brown Trout

They may be found in nearly freezing water...

PLATE 2
Arctic Char

or in warm tropical water.

Fish can breathe underwater because they have gills.

PLATE 4
Bluegill

Fins help them swim.

PLATE 5
Rainbow Darter

Most fish eat meat.

Fish are different shapes and sizes.

a.

b.

d.

They protect themselves in many ways.

Most have tough skin covered by scales.

The skin of a fish is slippery.

PLATE 10
Chinook Salmon

Fish may be colored to look like their surroundings…

Plate 11
Pacific Halibut

or marked in other ways that fool their enemies.

Plate 12
Foureye Butterflyfish

Many fish live together in groups called schools.

PLATE 13
Lookdown

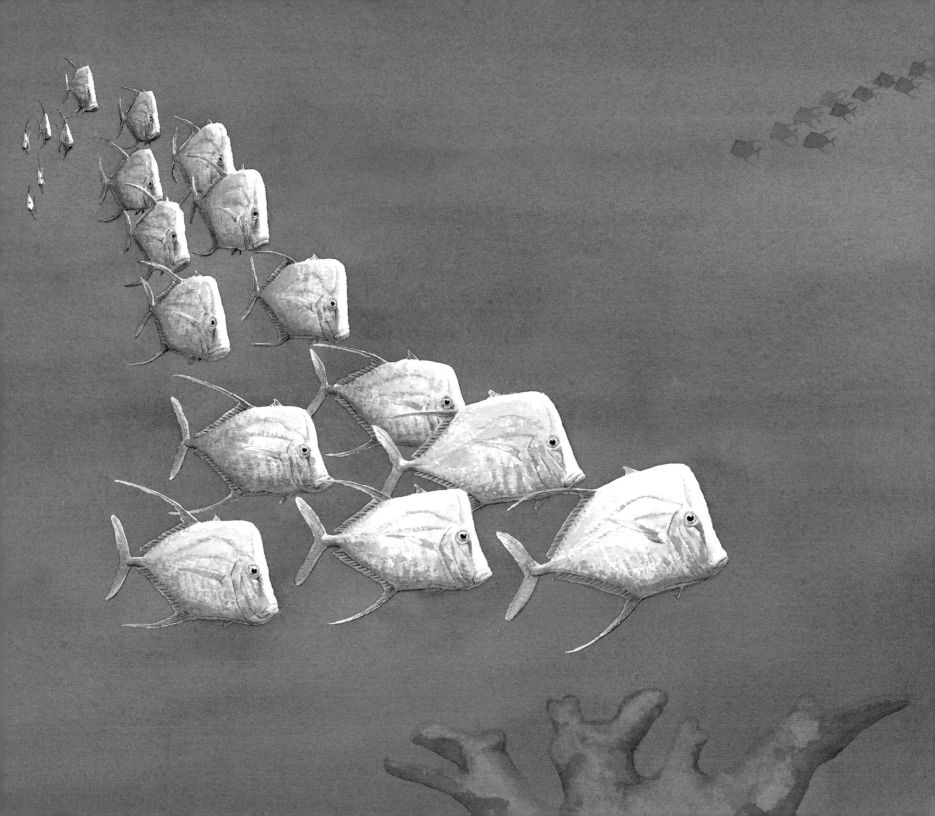

A few kinds of fish defend themselves with venomous spines.

Some baby fish are born alive. Other baby fish hatch from eggs laid by the mother.

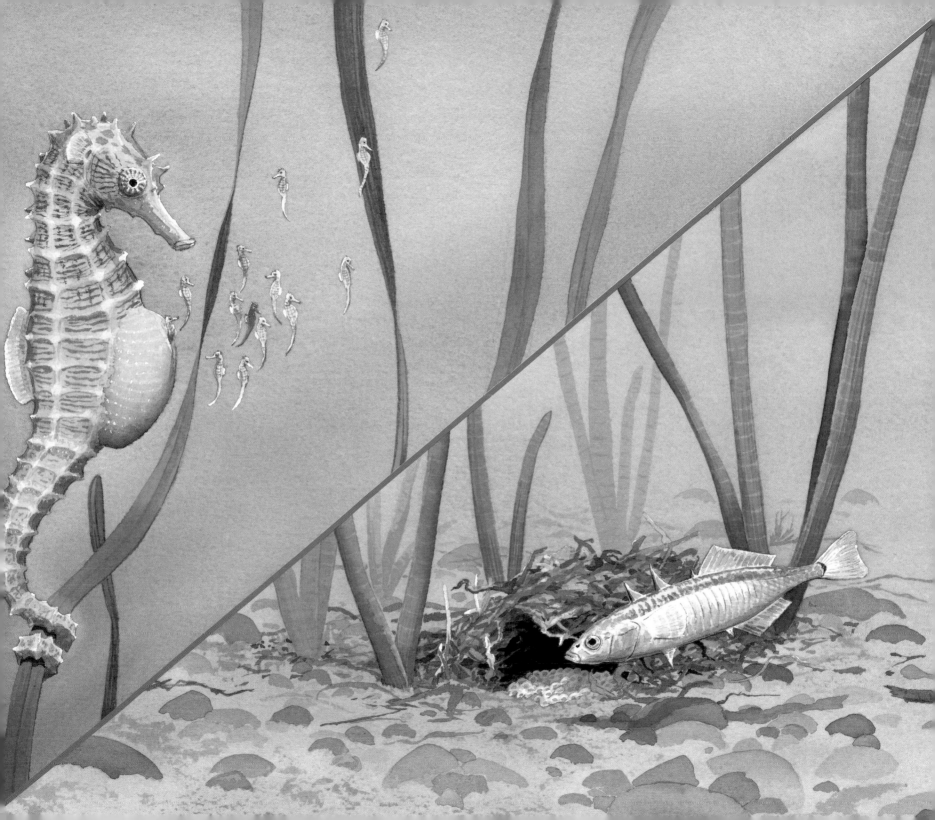

Fish keep growing as long as they live.

Fish provide food, jobs, and recreation for many people.

It is important to protect fish and the places where they live.

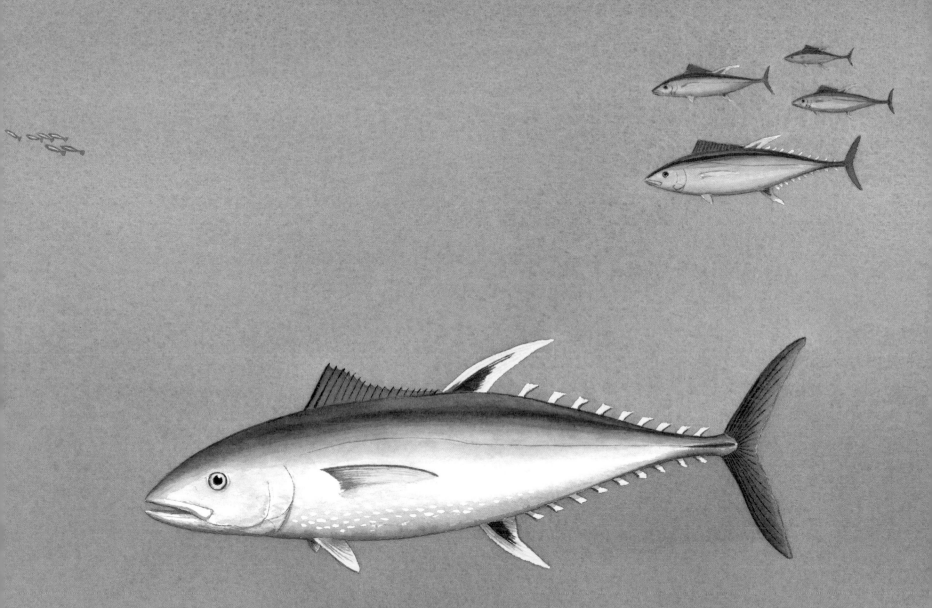

Afterword

PLATE 1
Scientists estimate that there are over 30,000 different species of fish.* They live in almost all fresh and salt waters in the world. Most fish live in a specific habitat, and only a few species move between oceans and rivers. Brown Trout are native to rivers and streams of Europe, northern Africa, and western Asia. They were introduced to North America in 1883.

PLATE 2
Fish are able to survive in freezing water by staying underneath the ice. There they become less active and do not need as much food. The colder waters of the world have fewer species of fish than tropical or temperate waters. Arctic Char live in cold fresh and salt waters of the Arctic. Those that live in the ocean migrate to freshwater lakes and rivers to lay their eggs. They live the farthest north of any freshwater fish.

PLATE 3
Fish that live in tropical waters are generally more brightly colored than those found in cooler waters. Brilliant colors and bold patterns help them blend in with the light and shadows of their environment. The vivid blues and yellows of the Queen Angelfish are hard for predators to see against colorful coral reefs. They live in warm parts of the western Atlantic Ocean.

*Note: Scientific guides generally use the plural form "fishes" when referring to a number of different species. For the sake of simplicity, we have chosen the use the plural form "fish."

PLATE 4

Like all animals, fish need to breathe oxygen. They have gills for breathing instead of lungs. Fish gulp water through their mouths. As the water flows over their gills, the oxygen is removed. The water then goes out through openings on the sides of their heads. Many fish have a bony flap that covers and protects their gills. Bluegills get their name from the blue tab on their gill flaps. They are common in lakes, ponds, and streams in North America.

PLATE 5

Fins help fish move through the water. They use them to steer, balance, and stop. Darters are small fish that move by using their fins to "dart about." Rainbow Darters live in small, clean streams and rivers in North America. They are easily harmed by pollution. Mud, and silt in the water can smother their eggs and cover their food supplies.

PLATE 6

Many fish eat other fish. They also eat worms, insects, shellfish, and other water animals. A few eat water plants. Largemouth Bass eat other fish, crayfish, insects, frogs, and even baby ducks and small mammals. They are a popular freshwater game fish in North America.

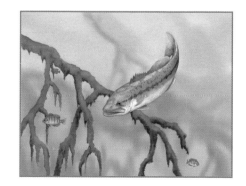

PLATE 7

Fish are shaped for where they live and what they eat. Flat fish such as Bluespotted Ribbontail Rays have mouths on the underside of their bodies so they can scoop up food from the ocean floor. Powder Blue Tangs and other reef fish have thin bodies so they can make sharp turns in coral reefs. White Sturgeon, the largest freshwater fish in North America, grow up to 20 feet (6 meters) long. Neon Tetras are around 1½ inches (4 centimeters) long.

PLATE 8

Since all but the largest fish are in danger of being eaten by predators, they need ways of protecting themselves. Porcupinefish swallow water or air and inflate like a balloon. The raised spines and puffed-up body make a prickly mouthful that is hard for other fish and animals to swallow. Spot-fin Porcupinefish live in the Pacific and Atlantic Oceans.

PLATE 9

Scales help protect the skin of fish from injury. Some species of fish have scales that are smooth and flat. Others have scales that are rough like tiny teeth. A few kinds of fish do not have scales. The heavy, diamond-shaped scales of Longnose Gar offer protection from most predators. Gars live in lakes, slow-moving streams, and estuaries in the eastern United States.

PLATE 10

Special glands in the skin of fish produce a slimy substance that helps them move easily through the water. This mucus also protects fish from parasites and infections. Salmon migrate from the ocean to rivers to spawn or lay their eggs. The Chinook (or King) Salmon is the largest type of salmon. Chinooks can weigh up to 100 pounds (45.3 kilograms).

PLATE 11

Flatfish—including halibut, flounder, and sole—swim on their sides along the ocean floor. They are not born flat. As flatfish grow, their bodies change shape and their eyes move to one side of their heads. They are camouflaged to match their habitat. Pacific Halibut are a valuable commercial fish that can grow to nearly 9 feet (2.7 meters) and weigh up to 800 pounds (363 kilograms). They live in the North Pacific Ocean.

PLATE 12

Some fish have patterns on their bodies that are confusing to predators and prey. The black eyespot on the rear of the Foureye Butterflyfish and the black stripe through its eye make it hard to tell if the fish is coming or going. Foureye Butterflyfish live in the western Atlantic Ocean from the United States to northern South America.

PLATE 13

Fish travel in schools to take advantage of "safety in numbers." It can be hard for a predator to pick out a single fish when a group is swimming together in the same direction. Schooling may also make it easier for the fish to find food and mates. Lookdowns are hard to see head-on because their bodies are very thin and flat. They live in the western Atlantic Ocean along the coasts of North and South America.

PLATE 14

Venomous animals inject toxin (a poisonous substance) into other animals. When threatened, Stonefish use needlelike spines located on their backs to sting enemies. Stonefish are thought to be the most venomous fish in the world. They live in tropical waters of the Indian and Pacific Oceans.

PLATE 15

Some fish carry eggs inside their bodies until the babies are ready to be born. A female seahorse lays her eggs in a special pouch on the male's belly. He keeps the eggs in this brood pouch until they hatch and pop out. The male Threespine Stickleback makes a nest from vegetation, where the female lays her eggs. He guards the eggs until they hatch and stays with the young until they can take care of themselves. Not all fish guard their eggs and young. Lined Seahorses live in the western Atlantic Ocean. Threespine Sticklebacks live in North America, Europe, and parts of Asia in salt water and freshwater.

PLATE 16

The scales of most fish grow as the animal gets older. It is sometimes possible to tell the age of a fish by counting the growth rings on its scales. Whale Sharks, the largest fish in the world, may grow to over 40 feet (12 meters) in length. They eat tiny shrimp and fish that they strain from the ocean water. Whale Sharks are harmless to people. They live in oceans all over the world.

PLATE 17

Fish are an enormously important source of food for other animals as well as for people. Fishing done in a responsible way has little impact on the environment. Laws are needed to keep people from catching too many fish. Some fishing methods unintentionally kill other animals and fish. These accidents (called "bycatch") need to be prevented. Some fish populations have been reduced to dangerously low numbers because of overfishing.

PLATE 18

Pollution from many different sources harms fish in oceans, rivers, and lakes. Dangerous chemicals from industry and agriculture, silt caused by erosion, and garbage dumped by people cause problems for fish all over the world. We need to protect fish by keeping our waterways clean. Yellowfin Tuna are a valuable food fish and prized game fish. Scientists are concerned that their numbers are declining because of overfishing. Yellowfin Tuna are found in tropical waters of oceans around the world.

GLOSSARY

camouflage—colors or patterns on an animal that help it hide

game fish—fish caught for recreation or sport

habitat—the place where animals and plants live and grow

parasite—an animal or plant that lives on or inside another animal or plant

predator—an animal that lives by hunting and eating other animals

prey—an animal that is hunted and eaten by a predator

species—a group of animals or plants that are alike in many ways

temperate—not very hot and not very cold

tropical—the area near the equator that is hot year-round

SUGGESTIONS FOR FURTHER READING

Books

EYEWITNESS BOOKS: FISH by Steve Parker (DK Publishing)

A PLACE FOR FISH by Melissa Stewart (Peachtree Publishers)

ANIMAL CLASSIFICATIONS: FISH by Angela Royston (Heinemann Raintree)

FISH FACTS by Geoff Swinney (Pelican Publishing Company)

Websites

Fish FAQ
www.nefsc.noaa.gov/faq

Wildscreen Archive
www.arkive.org/fish

Ducksters
www.ducksters.com/animals/fish.php

ABOUT... SERIES

HC: 978-1-68263-031-0
PB: 978-1-68263-032-7

HC: 978-1-56145-038-1
PB: 978-1-56145-364-1

HC: 978-1-56145-688-8
PB: 978-1-56145-699-4

HC: 978-1-56145-301-6
PB: 978-1-56145-405-1

HC: 978-1-56145-987-2
PB: 978-1-56145-988-9

HC: 978-1-56145-588-1
PB: 978-1-56145-837-0

HC: 978-1-56145-881-3
PB: 978-1-56145-882-0

HC: 978-1-56145-757-1
PB: 978-1-56145-758-8

HC: 978-1-56145-906-3

HC: 978-1-56145-358-0
PB: 978-1-56145-407-5

PB: 978-1-56145-406-8

HC: 978-1-56145-795-3

HC: 978-1-56145-743-4
PB: 978-1-56145-741-0

HC: 978-1-56145-536-2
PB: 978-1-56145-811-0

HC: 978-1-56145-907-0
PB: 978-1-56145-908-7

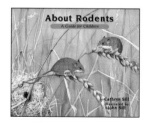
HC: 978-1-56145-454-9
PB: 978-1-56145-914-8

HC: 978-1-68263-004-4

ALSO AVAILABLE IN SPANISH AND ENGLISH/SPANISH EDITIONS

● About Amphibians / Sobre los anfibios / 978-1-68263-033-4 PB ● About Birds / Sobre los pájaros / 978-1-56145-783-0 PB ● Sobre los pájaros / 978-1-68263-071-6 PB ● About Fish / Sobre los peces / 978-1-56145-989-6 PB ● About Insects / Sobre los insectos / 978-1-56145-883-7 PB ● About Mammals / Sobre los mamíferos / 978-1-56145-800-4 PB ● Sobre los mamíferos / 978-1-68263-072-3 PB ● About Reptiles / Sobre los reptiles / 978-1-56145-909-4 PB

ABOUT HABITATS SERIES

Deserts

HC: 978-1-56145-641-3
PB: 978-1-56145-636-9

Forests

HC: 978-1-56145-734-2
PB: 978-1-68263-126-3

Grasslands

HC: 978-1-56145-559-1
PB: 978-1-68263-034-1

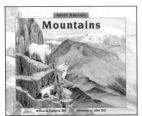

Mountains

HC: 978-1-56145-469-3
PB: 978-1-56145-731-1

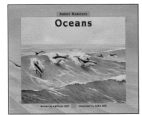

Oceans

HC: 978-1-56145-618-5
PB: 978-1-56145-960-5

Polar Regions

HC: 978-1-56145-832-5

Seashores

HC: 978-1-56145-968-1

Wetlands

HC: 978-1-56145-432-7
PB: 978-1-56145-689-5

THE SILLS

CATHRYN AND JOHN SILL are the dynamic team who created the *About…* series as well as the *About Habitats* series. Their books have garnered praise from educators and have won a variety of awards, including Bank Street Best Books, CCBC Choices, NSTA/CBC Outstanding Science Trade Books for Students K–12, Orbis Pictus Recommended, and *Science Books and Films* Best Books of the Year. Cathryn, a graduate of Western Carolina State University, taught early elementary school classes for thirty years. John holds a BS in wildlife biology from North Carolina State University. Combining his artistic skill and knowledge of wildlife, he has achieved an impressive reputation as a wildlife artist. The Sills live in Franklin, North Carolina.